RENEGADE GOSPEL

YOUTH STUDY BOOK

Renegade Gospel
The Rebel Jesus

Book

978-1-4267-9279-3

978-1-4267-9280-9 eBook

DVD

978-1-4267-9282-3

Leader Guide

978-1-4267-9281-6

978-1-63088-037-8 eBook

Youth Study Book

978-1-4267-9283-0

978-1-4267-9284-7 eBook

Children's Leader Guide

978-1-4267-9285-4

For more information, visit www.MikeSlaughter.com

Also by Mike Slaughter

Dare to Dream
shiny gods
Christmas Is Not Your Birthday
Change the World
Spiritual Entrepreneurs
Real Followers
Momentum for Life
UnLearning Church
Upside Living in a Downside Economy

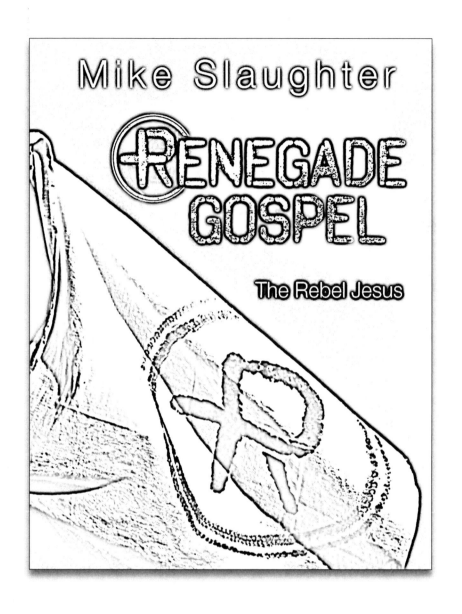

Mike Slaughter

RENEGADE GOSPEL

The Rebel Jesus

YOUTH STUDY BOOK

BY JENNY YOUNGMAN

Abingdon Press / Nashville

RENEGADE GOSPEL: The Rebel Jesus

Youth Study Book
by Jenny Youngman

This book is printed on elemental chlorine-free paper.

ISBN 978-1-4267-9283-0

14 15 16 17 18 19 20 21 22 23—10 9 8 7 6 5 4 3 2 1

MANUFACTURED IN THE UNITED STATES OF AMERICA

CONTENTS

INTRODUCTION

Have you ever wondered why the pictures of Jesus hanging in children's Sunday school classrooms portray a blond-haired, blue-eyed dude in a gown, carrying a smiling sheep? Me too! But you know what? That's not the real Jesus. Sure, it's sweet to think of Jesus as an uber-friendly, never-gets-mad character, but it's just not the truth. Jesus was a rebel. He was a revolutionary. He turned the world upside down, and his teachings threatened the powers of the day. Somehow we've watered down Jesus and fashioned him into a portrait that might be hung in an art gallery. We've made him manageable, nice, and safe. But that's not how it all went down.

Actually, Jesus was a member of a marginalized and persecuted minority. Mike Slaughter, pastor and author of *Renegade Gospel*, writes that Jesus "spent the first two years of his life as a refugee in Africa due to the campaign of genocide initiated by King Herod. His mission was seen as heretical by the religiously correct and as subversive by the Roman political forces that occupied Palestine. Tradition tells us that all his disciples, except the Apostle John who died in exile on the Island of Patmos, suffered martyrs' deaths for their allegiance to this man and his mission. They were convinced he was Lord (the ultimate authority) above all other religious and political systems in the world.

Their unwavering allegiance was based on their firm conviction that he was raised bodily from the dead."

This Lenten season, let's not just hear the story of Jesus' death and resurrection, eat our Easter candy, and get on with normal life. What if we could be radically changed by this rebel called Jesus? What if we took his teachings seriously in our daily lives? What if we lived believing he is alive and living in and through us? It's easy to say yes to Jesus' call. It's not as easy to follow him wherever he leads. During the Lenten season, Jesus leads us to Calvary and asks us to lay down our lives, take up our cross, and follow him to a life of true discipleship.

This book will help us take a good, long look at Jesus and see who he really was, what he really was about, and what it really means to follow him. There is no better time than now, in this Lenten season, to begin following Jesus. My prayer is that you will bring all you've ever thought, wondered, or doubted about Jesus and invite him to show you who he is—and that you'll say *Yes!* and follow hard after him.

TO THE LEADER

As you lead a group through this book, you will want to be sure each student has his or her own book to read and write in. Each chapter is divided into seven sections that are described below. You may want to read Mike Slaughter's book *Renegade Gospel* as a resource, but it is not required as this book is meant to stand on its own.

Watch the Video (Optional)
Renegade Gospel includes a DVD with six videos, one per chapter, of Mike Slaughter discussing the rebel Jesus with a small group from his church. The videos were originally produced for adults, but Slaughter's edgy, challenging style is in many ways ideal for youth. If you decide to use the videos, begin each session by showing the video segment. These videos introduce the topic and scriptural emphasis and will serve as an excellent introduction and backdrop for your session.

Share in Conversation
Use these questions as icebreakers to get people talking and to transition into deeper conversation and discussion.

Read and Reflect
If you have a group of readers, you may want to ask students to read this section aloud. If you prefer, review this section ahead of time and highlight the main points for the group.

Scripture Focus
This is the primary Scripture passage for the session. Have someone read it aloud or read it aloud together as a group.

Check in with Mike Slaughter
These are adapted excerpts from Mike Slaughter's book *Renegade Gospel* that emphasize the biblical teaching for each session. Review the material and the Scripture text with your group and discuss the questions.

Go Deeper
These questions will bring together the video, Scriptures, and readings and will invite students to begin applying it to their lives.

Make a Jesus Mural
The hoped-for outcome of this book is for young people to discover the real Jesus and say yes to following him wherever he leads. In this section, youth will work together to make a graffiti mural to hang in the youth room. They will add to the mural each week. For this ongoing activity you will need a large, wall-size canvas sheet, a tarp, spray paint, black permanent markers, and an open area. Paint (or have an artistic youth paint) the word *Jesus* in block, graffiti-style letters in the middle of the canvas sheet. Students will add words and images onto the sheet each week as they discover more about the rebel Jesus.

Listen for God
Each chapter concludes with a prayer. You can use this prayer, substitute one of your own, or design a prayer activity that includes the group.

1.

DISCOVERING THE
REBEL JESUS

Then he said to them all: "Whoever wants to be my disciple must deny themselves and take up their cross daily and follow me. For whoever wants to save their life will lose it, but whoever loses their life for me will save it. What good is it for someone to gain the whole world, and yet lose or forfeit their very self?" (Luke 9:23-25)

1.

DISCOVERING THE REBEL JESUS

Watch the Video (Optional)

If your group is using the Renegade Gospel DVD, watch the DVD segment for Session 1, titled "Discovering the Rebel Jesus." Then reflect on the following questions and make some notes. If you are in a group setting, use the questions to discuss the video.

Share in Conversation

1. How would you describe and summarize the Jesus you learned about as a child?

2. How would you describe Jesus to someone who didn't know anything about him?

3. What does the word *rebel* mean to you?

4. Why do you think Jesus could be described as a rebel?

Read and Reflect

As we grow and mature, so many things about our lives change. Things we took for granted as children become questions that need answers, and things we thought we believed nag at us for evidence or some proof. If you grew up in a churchgoing family, you may have a set of beliefs that you've learned about what it means to be a Christian. If you are new to the faith, you may be wondering what this Christian thing is all about. This book will challenge both lifelong believers and new seekers to take a good, long look at Jesus, and then take the step forward to follow hard after him. In the end, you'll find a faith in Jesus that is worth staking your whole life upon.

The Jesus on the Wall

If you took a quick tour around your church's Sunday school rooms or flipped through the pages of your children's Bible, you might find some pictures of Jesus in his safe, European-looking, docile depictions. Blond hair, blue eyes, glowing face—you know the one. The truth is that we aren't sure what Jesus looked like. Artists throughout history have painted images of Jesus, then added their own cultural or physical traits. In the same way that pictures on the wall can get Jesus wrong, sometimes Christians can get Jesus' teachings wrong, really wrong. Oftentimes, Jesus gets confused with a super-sweet angel or a big fun brother instead of the radical, revolutionary leader of a movement that he was. To a world that was politically corrupt, where justice was relative, where rights were ignored, Jesus spoke about a new kind of kingdom where the last are first, the lowly are lifted up, and the poor are blessed. Radical stuff!

So, what does Jesus have to say in our world, in which there are laws, accountability for leaders, and guaranteed rights? Is Jesus' radical message still relevant today? You bet it is. As I write this, an unarmed African-American teenager has been shot and killed by a police officer. Racial tensions and mistrust of government are thick in the air. What does the rebel Jesus have to say to the rioting crowds and the defensive governmental officials?

On the other side of the world, in the Middle East, a terrorist group has begun a genocide, forcing refugees into the desert mountains to starve or die of thirst. The international community is sending aid as they can, but families are wondering if help will come in time. What does the rebel Jesus say to those of us who look on in horror, feeling helpless to effect change in such a situation?

As a final example—only for the sake of space, not because there aren't more—South and Central American parents are sending their kids to the United States in order to save them from drug lords, gangs, and extreme poverty. If their kids can just get across the border, they think, the kids will have a chance at a better life. American citizens are in opposing camps about this issue, and views run the spectrum from "round them up and send them back" to "get them some food and a place to sleep, then we'll sort it all out." What does the rebel Jesus say to the parents who take such a risk and to those in the U.S. who grapple with the issue?

How does the rebel Jesus speak to the issues of our day?

Unwatering the Gospel

I use these examples of current events because, if we're not careful, our faith can turn stale and we can become what Mike Slaughter calls the "frozen chosen." Those are Christians who think the church is a building where you go once a week and then leave without a thought about living as true disciples of Jesus Christ. Sometimes our youth groups can do this—we show up for great music, an inspiring talk, and some hang-out time with friends, but we leave without any thoughts about what it really means to follow Jesus.

What this world needs is not a building full of Christians with their hands in the air, but a bunch of Christians who are willing to follow Jesus into the world with hands reaching out. The world needs our faith to matter to us and needs our feet to put that faith into action.

The true gospel of Jesus isn't watered down; it isn't safe. His message was a threat to the religious leaders and government officials of his time, and his message might just feel a little threatening to the church today if we took him seriously. Remember, Jesus didn't come to start a religion, but to start a countercultural revolution that we are invited to be a part of. So, let's take a close look to discover the rebel Jesus and what it means to follow him.

Scripture Focus

Once when Jesus was praying in private and his disciples were with him, he asked them, "Who do the crowds say I am?"

They replied, "Some say John the Baptist; others say Elijah; and still others, that one of the prophets of long ago has come back to life."

"But what about you?" he asked. "Who do you say I am?"

Peter answered, "God's Messiah."

Jesus strictly warned them not to tell this to anyone. And he said, "The Son of Man must suffer many things and be rejected by the elders, the chief priests and the teachers of the law, and he must be killed and on the third day be raised to life."

Then he said to them all: "Whoever wants to be my disciple must deny themselves and take up their cross daily and follow me. For whoever wants to save their life will lose it, but whoever loses their life for me will save it. What good is it for someone to gain the whole world, and yet lose or forfeit their very self? Whoever is ashamed of me and my words, the Son of Man will be ashamed of them when he comes in his glory and in the glory of the Father and of the holy angels.

"Truly I tell you, some who are standing here will not taste death before they see the kingdom of God." (Luke 9:18-27)

Check in with Mike Slaughter
From Chapter One of *Renegade Gospel*

Jesus didn't guarantee that his followers would have a trouble-free life. He taught them hard truths and made no promises to them about easy living. In

Luke 9:23-24, Jesus said, "Whoever wants to be my disciple must deny themselves and take up their cross daily and follow me. For whoever wants to save their life will lose it, but whoever loses their life for me will save it." Some were unwilling to pay the price. In the Gospel of Mark, we read about a rich young man who was eager to experience what Jesus was offering. When the young man asked what he must do to obtain eternal life, Jesus gave this unexpected response: "Go, sell everything you have and give to the poor, and you will have treasure in heaven. Then come, follow me" (Mark 10:21). As many other aspiring disciples would do, both during and following Jesus' ministry on earth, the man walked away.

Nineteenth-century British pastor Charles Spurgeon once noted, "There are no crown bearers in heaven that were not cross bearers on earth."[1] Dr. Martin Luther King, Jr., echoed a similar theme when he noted, "Christianity has always insisted that the cross we bear precedes the crown we wear."[2] These are not feel-good messages that will easily attract a crowd, and neither were the messages that Jesus offered. In John we read that many of Jesus' disciples, after listening to some of Jesus' difficult teachings, "turned back and no longer followed him" (John 6:66).

Claiming the rebel Jesus requires a radical reprioritization of all we deem valuable. In the case of the wealthy young man, the priorities to be reordered were money and possessions, but sometimes the demands were even greater. In Luke 14:26, Jesus warned the crowd, "If anyone comes to me and does not hate father and mother, wife and children, brothers and sisters—yes, even their own life—such a person cannot be my disciple." The rebel Jesus also requires reprioritization of our relationships. Certainly Jesus does not want me to "hate" Carolyn, my wife of forty-two years, or my children. Yet he makes it abundantly evident that my allegiance to him as Lord must supersede all else—and everyone else—in my life.

Go Deeper

1. What would you say you believe about Jesus right now?
2. How would you rate your willingness to follow the rebel Jesus on a scale of 1-5? (Where 1 is "going nowhere" and 5 is "Jesus is my best friend.")
3. A surprising character knew who Jesus was as he addressed the crowds. Look at Mark 1:21-28:

> They went to Capernaum, and when the Sabbath came, Jesus went into the synagogue and began to teach. The people were amazed at his teaching, because he taught them as one who had authority, not as the teachers of the law. Just then a man in their synagogue who was possessed by an impure spirit cried out, "What do you want with us, Jesus of Nazareth? Have you come to destroy us? I know who you are—the Holy One of God!"

> "Be quiet!" said Jesus sternly. "Come out of him!" The impure spirit shook the man violently and came out of him with a shriek.

> The people were all so amazed that they asked each other, "What is this? A new teaching—and with authority! He even gives orders to impure spirits and they obey him." News about him spread quickly over the whole region of Galilee.

4. Who declared that Jesus was sent from God?
5. The demon knew who Jesus was and what he was capable of. The demon believed, but was it a Jesus follower? No way! Christians can get stuck at the point of belief—but even demons believe. Why is it so easy for Christians to hold on to their beliefs instead of putting them into action and obeying Jesus' commands?
6. What are some examples of putting into action a belief in Jesus?
7. Jesus didn't guarantee his followers a trouble-free life. He taught hard truths and made no promises about easy living. Look at Luke 9:23-24; Mark 10:21; and John 6:66.

8. What is difficult about Jesus' teachings?
9. Why do you think some people who heard Jesus' teachings walked away from him?
10. How would you reprioritze your life so that Jesus would be at the top of the list?
11. What are you discovering about the rebel Jesus that is different from what you previously believed?

Make a Jesus Mural

Throughout these sessions, you will be creating a graffiti mural for your youth room. The mural will replace the safe, blue-eyed Jesus of your childhood and remind you of the real, rebel Jesus and the life he is calling you to. Each week, after study and discussion, you'll reflect on how Jesus is calling you to follow him more closely. Spend some time in personal reflection, using the questions below. Then, grab some spray paint or markers and add to the mural. Use some of the words and images you listed here to add to the mural.

- Review some of Jesus' radical teachings in these verses: Matthew 22:39; 20:16; 20:26; 18:3; John 14:6; 10:10; 14:12; Matthew 20:28. List any aspects of Jesus' character, teachings, or actions that jump out at you.
- List some words that describe the real, rebel Jesus.
- List some words that describe what it means to follow the rebel Jesus.
- What images come to mind when you think about following Jesus wherever he leads?
- How would your life be different if you began to follow the rebel Jesus?

Listen for God

Rebel Jesus, we confess that we have sanitized your call and played it safe. Help us to dig deep into your word and into conversation with you to discover who you really are, what you are about, and how you want us to live. Give us boldness and bravery to follow hard after you. Amen.

2.
REVOLUTIONARY LIFESTYLE

The Spirit of the Sovereign LORD is on me,
    because the LORD has anointed me
    to proclaim good news to the poor.
He has sent me to bind up the brokenhearted,
    to proclaim freedom for the captives
    and release from darkness for the prisoners. (Isaiah 61:1)

2.

REVOLUTIONARY LIFESTYLE

Watch the Video (Optional)

If your group is using the *Renegade Gospel* DVD, watch the DVD segment for Session 2, titled "Revolutionary Lifestyle." Then reflect on the following questions and make some notes. If you are in a group setting, use the questions to discuss the video.

Share in Conversation

1. When you think about Jesus' lifestyle, what comes to mind?

2. When you think about the stereotypical "Christian" lifestyle, what comes to mind?

3. How similar or dissimilar are your images of Jesus' lifestyle versus the typical Christian lifestyle? Why do you think this is?

4. How would you describe a "revolutionary lifestyle"?

Read and Reflect

How many words describe you? Student? Athlete? Musician? Actor? Republican? Democrat? Libertarian? Christian? The world has many words we can hang our hats on, and each word assumes a kind of lifestyle. If you are a student, you attend school, study and do homework at night, and participate to some degree in the life of the student community. If you are an athlete, you practice at least once a day, work out and maybe watch what you eat, strive for fitness goals and achievements in your sport. If you are a musician, you practice hours a day, listen to great music, and immerse yourself in your art.

But what about the lifestyle of a Christian? Off the top of our heads, we might say a Christian is someone who goes to church regularly, prays sometimes, and maybe participates in a class or Bible study. But is that really the lifestyle that Jesus modeled for his followers? Is that all we should be known for? Some people might say the Christian lifestyle is less about what we do and more about how we act—judgmental and hypocritical. Sadly, for too many of us that's an accurate description. We are so caught up in our church commitments that we forget to be the church—the hands and feet of Jesus. We have said yes to salvation and are safely hanging out with the saints until we go to heaven. We have made our faith personal and private instead of outward and radical. But if faith is only about "my salvation" and "my ticket to heaven," then we are getting it way wrong; our priorities are out of whack and need an adjustment.

See, Jesus came to lift up the poor, heal broken hearts, proclaim freedom for captives—to be about justice and mercy. His salvation is not about our getting a one-way ticket to heaven. We are saved from sin so that we might lead a life of discipleship, of mission, of walking with Jesus down the narrow road he talks about in Matthew 7:14.

Jesus was constantly challenging his followers to serve the poor, the oppressed, and the outcast. He told a rich young ruler in Mark 10:21 to sell everything he had and give it to the poor. In Matthew 7, he says that everyone who hears his words and actually puts his teachings into practice are like wise people who build their houses on rock so the houses can't be shaken by storms. He says in Matthew 5 that his followers are the salt and the light of the earth, the thing that preserves and gives flavor, the thing that is a beacon to all. Our task is to tell everyone, "Here! Here is the place where you can find justice, relief, mercy, hope, joy, freedom!" We are called to shine our lights and point people to God.

So, what does Christ's radical lifestyle look like? Even as young people—especially as young people—we can merge our personal salvation with the social, missional gospel of Jesus to show the world around us what God might look like. Following Jesus means making everything subject to God's authority in your life. It means that God has set you apart, has anointed you to proclaim a different kind of gospel in the world. When the world preaches health, wealth, and prosperity, the gospel of Jesus peaches wholeness, riches in glory, and generosity. When the world preaches despair, disappointment, and distrust, the gospel of Jesus preaches hope, grace, and faith.

A revolutionary lifestyle for you and for me means putting our allegiance to God first, before allegiance to our country, our wallets, and our culture. It means that we proclaim good news, and we work for justice and mercy for the oppressed. The church of Jesus Christ is not simply a gathering of believers huddled together until they get to heaven. Instead, the church of Jesus Christ is a gathering of called-out people who are all-in for the sake of Christ, for the bringing of his Kingdom on earth, and for the binding up of the brokenhearted here on earth.

So, how would you describe your life as a Christian now? Radical and revolutionary, or safe and predictable? Either way, I hope you'll ask Jesus to mess you up this Lent and call you deeper into life with him.

Scripture Focus

The Spirit of the Sovereign LORD is on me,
 because the LORD has anointed me
 to proclaim good news to the poor.
He has sent me to bind up the brokenhearted,
 to proclaim freedom for the captives
 and release from darkness for the prisoners,
to proclaim the year of the LORD's favor
 and the day of vengeance of our God,
to comfort all who mourn,
 and provide for those who grieve in Zion—

to bestow on them a crown of beauty
    instead of ashes,
the oil of joy
    instead of mourning,
and a garment of praise
    instead of a spirit of despair.
They will be called oaks of righteousness,
    a planting of the Lord
for the display of his splendor.

They will rebuild the ancient ruins
    and restore the places long devastated;
they will renew the ruined cities
    that have been devastated for generations. (Isaiah 61:1-4)

Check in with Mike Slaughter
From Chapter Two of *Renegade Gospel*

Christians have made the rebel Jesus into a "safe" Jesus, a Sunday school Jesus, and have stopped taking risks on behalf of the Kingdom. Since the third century, the church has moved from being a revolutionary movement to a museum for saints, much like many of the beautiful cathedrals that dot European cities. We need to become a radical, risk-taking community that once again reflects the directives of its renegade leader and passes the movement on to the next generations. Our call to a dangerous faith is one reason why I made sure my children were exposed to some of the world's hard and challenging places. When my son was a middle school student, I took him to the demilitarized zone between North and South Korea at a time when tensions were high between the two countries. In 2007, when my son was in his twenties, he traveled with me to the war zone of Darfur. When our children were young, my wife, Carolyn, and I took them both to Dachau, the first Nazi concentration camp, which opened in 1933 shortly after Adolf Hitler became chancellor of Germany. At Dachau, countless thousands of Jews and other prisoners were executed or died of malnutrition, disease, and overwork. We made a point of showing them the building where Christian prisoners were held after arrest for hiding Jews as part of a liberation movement. Now, as a grandparent, I hold myself accountable for making sure that my grandchildren also witness the risk and cost that may be required in following the rebel Jesus.

The Lenten season is the perfect time to reevaluate our lifestyle. During Lent, this season of introspection, we need to ask ourselves some challenging questions, both as individuals and as a church. Where have we accommodated our lives to worldly values instead of Kingdom values, to worldly politics instead of a new Kingdom community? What are we saying to our children? More importantly, what are we modeling to them? In what ways do we need to fast and to repent?

Challenging ourselves in this way is what the new birth in Jesus is all about. Being born again is like being transported from one kingdom, the kingdom of the world, to the kingdom of God. Yet we also have to give ourselves the same grace as Jesus extended to us. We are works in progress. At the time of our conversion, we basically say to Jesus, "I am all in, but I am not perfect." We must trust Jesus for our salvation, knowing that, left to our own devices and resources, we will never be good enough to have earned it. But our righteousness is not our own; our righteousness is in Christ and through what Jesus did for us in his death on the cross and resurrection. I have been walking with Jesus for more than forty years, and I am still in the process of detoxification from all that the world preaches and practices that does not reflect God's kingdom.

Go Deeper

1. How have Christians remade Jesus into our image?
2. What does it mean to put God first, above your allegiance to country?
3. How can we say "Jesus is Lord" and still love our country?
4. Take turns reading all of Matthew 5, paying close attention to each instruction. What words sum up the lifestyle that Jesus teaches?
5. What is revolutionary about the way Jesus told his followers to conduct themselves? How are his teachings different from what the world teaches?

6. Jesus' teachings are challenging, to say the least. Which of his instructions are the most difficult for you to put into practice?
7. What would the world look like if everyone who claims Jesus as Lord really lived the way he taught us to?

Make a Jesus Mural

Reflect on how Jesus is calling you to follow him more closely. Spend some time in personal reflection, using the questions below. Then grab some spray paint or markers and add to your Jesus mural. Use some of the words and images you listed here.

- Review some of Jesus' radical teachings in these verses: Matthew 5:3-10. List any aspects of Jesus' revolutionary lifestyle that jump out at you.
- List some words that describe what your life would look like if you took on Jesus' revolutionary lifestyle.
- List some words that describe what the world would look like if Christians put Jesus' lifestyle into practice.
- What images come to mind when you think about living out Jesus' revolutionary lifestyle?

Listen for God

Lord, in the midst of my doubt, skepticism, and uncertainty, I make the commitment today not only to confess you with my lips as Lord Jesus but to go where you are going and do what you are doing. I will leave no route for retreat or escape. I will be called by your name, and I will be numbered among your people. And it is in your name, Jesus, that I pray. Amen.

3.

THE MOST IMPORTANT QUESTION YOU WILL EVER HAVE TO ANSWER

Once when Jesus was praying by himself, the disciples joined him, and he asked them, "Who do the crowds say that I am?"

They answered, "John the Baptist, others Elijah, and still others that one of the ancient prophets has come back to life."

He asked them, "And what about you? Who do you say that I am?"

Peter answered, "The Christ sent from God." (Luke 9:18-20 CEB)

3.

THE MOST IMPORTANT QUESTION YOU WILL EVER HAVE TO ANSWER

Watch the Video (Optional)

If your group is using the *Renegade Gospel* DVD, watch the DVD segment for Session 3, titled "The Most Important Question You Will Ever Have to Answer." Then reflect on the following questions and make some notes. If you are in a group setting, use the questions to discuss the video.

Share in Conversation

1. If you asked random people on the street who Jesus is, what do you think they would say?
2. What would you say if someone stopped you to ask who Jesus is?
3. Why do you think some people have a hard time believing that Jesus is the Son of God?
4. What are some other doubts that people have that might keep them from believing Jesus is who he says he is?

5. When have you doubted something about God? How did you come to the point of faith? What doubts do you still have?

Read and Reflect

C. S. Lewis, author of the *Chronicles of Narnia*, was once a firm atheist until his friend J. R. R. Tolkien, author of the *Lord of the Rings Trilogy*, led him to Jesus. As Lewis took on the Christian life, he came to believe that ultimately we have to choose one of three differing beliefs about Jesus: (1) that he was a liar, which doesn't align with the high moral standard of his teachings; (2) that he was a lunatic who claimed to be God, which would be inconsistent because he actually demonstrated divine power on several occasions; and (3) that he was who he said he was—the Son of the living God, the Christ. In short, according to Lewis, the choice about who we believe Jesus to be is either liar, lunatic, or Lord.

Skeptics say that Jesus is a myth, but if you think about it, even the secular world is marked by signs of Jesus. For example, the calendar system we have used for thousands of years is based on the birth, death, and resurrection of Jesus. The term B.C. is an abbreviation for "Before Christ" and is used to denote years or time periods that occurred before Jesus' birth. The term A.D. stands for "anno Domini," which is Latin for "in the year of our Lord" and denotes time periods that fall after Jesus' birth.

Other skeptics say there is no proof to support the events of the Bible, but several reliable historical documents mention both Jesus and his followers. Some people deny the divinity of Jesus, saying it's too great a scientific leap—a transcendent God is just too bizarre an idea to believe when compared with the answers offered by science.

So, what do you believe about Jesus? Was he liar, lunatic, or Lord? Was he simply a great teacher who perhaps was a little too full of himself and claimed to be God? Was he a crazy dude with a skewed sense of reality and a narcissistic personality? Is he the Son of God and the Son of Man—completely human, completely divine—the Lord of Lords? If he is, what does that mean for those who claim his lordship?

Jesus' followers, his disciples, called him Rabbi. He was their teacher, and they were his students. They hung on his every word, followed him around, imitated him, spoke like him, took on his mannerisms. They wanted to soak in every moment they had with him. They wanted to be like him in every way possible, and so they said yes when he invited them to follow. His teachings weren't easy, and they required great sacrifice for those who said yes to his invitation.

Here's the thing for us today: We have a lot of choices in this world about what or whom to follow. We can go about life the way we want it, making decisions only for ourselves and our own advantage. We can say that Jesus is not who he says he is. We can make idols of anything and everything we want. We have the same choices about our belief in Jesus that Lewis wrote about. Do we call Jesus liar, lunatic, or Lord?

If Jesus is the Lord of our lives, then our choices, our words, our actions begin to look like his. He becomes our teacher and friend—the one with whom we want to soak up every minute and hang on every word. If Jesus is the Lord of our lives, then we take on his radical lifestyle, loving our enemies, giving away our stuff, offering grace instead of revenge, yielding our first-place spot to someone who needs it more. We say no to destructive lifestyles, and we say yes to freedom, generosity, joy, and abundant life. We say no to injustice, oppression, and despair, and we say yes to justice for all, release for captives, and hope against hope. It's all about the most important question you will ever have to answer: Who do you say Jesus is? Everything else about your life is based on your answer to that question.

Scripture Focus

Once when Jesus was praying by himself, the disciples joined him, and he asked them, "Who do the crowds say that I am?"

They answered, "John the Baptist, others Elijah, and still others that one of the ancient prophets has come back to life."

He asked them, "And what about you? Who do you say that I am?"

Peter answered, "The Christ sent from God." (Luke 9:18-20 CEB)

Check in with Mike Slaughter
From Chapter Three of *Renegade Gospel*

We struggle to follow Jesus, in part because our contemporary culture is saturated in a secular worldview. In this worldview, we operate as if God were not a factor. Jesus becomes a Sunday morning habit, and the rest of the week we seem to get along just fine without him. A secular worldview is also a materialistic worldview. We draw our security from our money and material possessions rather than from the promises of God. . . .

If we are going to follow Jesus, recognizing Jesus as Messiah, we will have to radically realign our life priorities. Jesus brilliantly illustrated this in a parable found in Luke 14:16-24. Jesus described a man, representing God, who is hosting a large dinner and sends out his servants to invite guests to the party. One by one the excuses come back from the invited guests. One invitee indicates that he has just bought a farm and needs to examine his new land. A second has bought five teams of oxen and feels compelled to see if they are working out as planned. A third invitee claims that he has just gotten married and is still on his honeymoon. Notice that the three invitees use the same excuses we give when we choose to revere Jesus instead of following him: our material property, our work, and our relationships. These convenient excuses betray our real allegiances and show that we relegate Jesus to someone we worship at church one morning a week. We have reduced the true worship of Jesus to singing three praise and worship songs on Sunday mornings. In the Bible, God's people sang songs in front of Israel's armies as they marched off to war, not when sitting in religious meetings. What happened to the practice of following Jesus sacrificially?

One thing I know: each of us in our lifetime will answer Jesus' question, "Who do you say that I am?"

Go Deeper

1. Why do you think Jesus asked the disciples the question, "Who do you say that I am?"
2. Have you ever doubted that Jesus is who he says he is? Where do you think doubt comes from? How can we overcome our doubts?
3. Look at Luke 9:1-2:

When Jesus had called the Twelve together, he gave them power and authority to drive out all demons and to cure diseases, and he sent them out to proclaim the kingdom of God and to heal the sick.

4. In the passage, what did Jesus give his followers the power to do?
5. How does that passage point to the need for believers to be in community as we do the work of the Kingdom?
6. Look at Colossians 1:15-18, sometimes called "The Christ Hymn":

The Son is the image of the invisible God, the firstborn over all creation. For in him all things were created: things in heaven and on earth, visible and invisible, whether thrones or powers or rulers or authorities; all things have been created through him and for him. He is before all things, and in him all things hold together. And he is the head of the body, the church; he is the beginning and the firstborn from among the dead, so that in everything he might have the supremacy.

7. What does this passage say about who Jesus is?
8. What does it mean that Christ has supremacy?
9. Look at this quote from Mike Slaughter:

When I confess that Jesus Christ is the Messiah, the Son of God, I commit to follow Jesus in a lifestyle of sacrificial service, walking in the dust of my Rabbi. Whatever my Rabbi values, I value. Whatever my Rabbi thinks about God, I think about God.

Whatever my Rabbi thinks about people, I think about people. Whatever my Rabbi believes about wealth, I believe about wealth. Whatever my Rabbi believes about the poor, I believe about the poor. Whatever my Rabbi believes about creation, I believe about creation. I act like my Rabbi, talk like my Rabbi, love like my Rabbi, and give my life away for my Rabbi's mission.

Unfortunately, many of us start that journey with enthusiasm but fail to sustain it. Our faith goes on cruise control as we start seeking comfort and not a calling.

10. How are you challenged by these words? What do you need to regroup, reprioritize, or refocus on during this Lenten season?

Make a Jesus Mural

Reflect on how Jesus is calling you to follow him more closely. Spend some time in personal reflection, using the suggestion below. Then, grab some spray paint or markers and add to the mural. Use some of the words and images you listed here on the mural.

Review the words of the Apostles' Creed, Ecumenical Version,[3] shown below. Slowly, read through each line and put the creed into your own words as you consider what to add to your mural.

> I believe in God, the Father Almighty,
>   creator of heaven and earth.
>
> I believe in Jesus Christ, his only Son, our Lord,
>   who was conceived by the Holy Spirit,
>   born of the Virgin Mary,
>   suffered under Pontius Pilate,
>   was crucified, died, and was buried;
>   he descended to the dead.

On the third day he rose again;
he ascended into heaven,
is seated at the right hand of the Father,
and will come again to judge the living and the dead.

I believe in the Holy Spirit,
the holy catholic* church,
the communion of saints,
the forgiveness of sins,
the resurrection of the body,
and the life everlasting. Amen.

*universal

Listen for God

Jesus, you are the Lord of Lords. You are the Beginning and the End. You are Son of God and Son of Man. You are our Rabbi, our Teacher, our Leader. We declare today that you are our Lord and we will follow you to the ends of the earth. We will do your work to bring the Kingdom here on earth. We will study your teachings, listen for your word, and go where you send us. Amen.

4.
SEEING JESUS
TODAY

"Though seeing, they do not see;
though hearing, they do not hear or understand." (Matthew 13:13)

4.
SEEING JESUS TODAY

Watch the Video (Optional)

If your group is using the *Renegade Gospel* DVD, watch the DVD segment for Session 4, titled "Seeing Jesus Today." Then reflect on the following questions and make some notes. If you are in a group setting, use the questions to discuss the video.

Share in Conversation

1. Tell about a time when you physically stumbled or tripped because you weren't looking where you were going.
2. How easy is it to get caught up in what we've got going on and completely miss out on something great? Think of an example from your own life.
3. Have you ever heard the phrase "missed the forest for the trees"? What does it mean?
4. When have you ever missed the forest for the trees?
5. Do you think there is a difference between looking versus seeing or hearing versus understanding? What is the difference?

Read and Reflect

Have you ever seen one of those art prints that can be interpreted as two different images, depending on the way you look at it? I have to admit, I can't stand those things! Whenever someone shows one to me, I usually am baffled. It seems like everyone around me can see both images, and I can barely make out one of them. I just do not have eyes to see those tricky art pieces, and they cause me great frustration.

Sometimes, seeing Jesus in the world today can be like those images. We can get lost in all the patterns of the world and lose sight of his path. We can squint and furrow our brow, tilt our head and push our hair back, but still we can't make out the footsteps of Jesus and the road he is leading us down. Sometimes it feels like everyone around us can see except us!

But we've got to know that our inability to see isn't about Jesus hiding from us or trying to trick us by looking like something else. If we don't see Jesus, it's because we aren't really looking. Last week we explored a question: "Who is Jesus?" This week let's think about another question: "Where is Jesus?" Jesus is not sitting idly by in the heavens waiting for the moment he makes his comeback. Jesus is alive and among us, and he tells us he is the least, the last, and the lost.

Think about the story of the sheep and the goats in Matthew 25. Jesus tells his followers that those who will inherit the Kingdom are those who fed the hungry, clothed the naked, gave water to the thirsty, invited strangers into their homes, cared for the sick and the imprisoned. He says whatever we did for the least among us, we did for him. If we want to find Jesus today, I think this parable tells us where to look: he's in the places where he calls us to serve.

In order to see Jesus today, we have to look for him with expectation, fully believing that we will find him. But here's the thing. If the Jesus we're looking for is the blond-haired, blue-eyed, safe-and-sound Jesus hanging as a portrait in our Sunday school rooms, we're not going to find him. We won't find him in our childlike storybook imagination. Remember, Jesus was a revolutionary. He was a game-changer. He was a rebel. If we want to see him in the world, we need to look up and invite him to give us eyes to see the world the way he does.

When we pray, "Give me your eyes," Jesus will show us so that we really see what he cares about and experience a softening of our hearts for the things that break his heart. He will reveal miracles all around us.

In order to know Jesus today, we have to pray for eyes to see and ears to hear. Jesus told his followers in Matthew 13:13-15 that he speaks in parables so that we can hear and understand. He wants our hearts to be good soil in which his word can sink deep, grow roots, and become a mighty tree. Is that you? Are you open to seeing Jesus as he works in and through and all around you? Are your eyes and ears open to see, hear, and understand?

Personally, I have to pray to avoid spiritual drowsiness, laziness, and apathy. I have to pray to ask God to keep my lamp trimmed and burning with the expectation of seeing him. I have to pray to stay awake when he asks me to keep watch. We are coworkers with Christ, bringing his kingdom on earth as it is in heaven. Expect to see him. Invite him to open your eyes and heart this Lent. Watch to see him do a new thing in and through you.

Scripture Focus

"Though seeing, they do not see;
   though hearing, they do not hear or understand.

"In them is fulfilled the prophecy of Isaiah:

"'You will be ever hearing but never understanding;
   you will be ever seeing but never perceiving.
For this people's heart has become calloused;
   they hardly hear with their ears,
   and they have closed their eyes.
Otherwise they might see with their eyes,
   hear with their ears,
   understand with their hearts
and turn, and I would heal them.'" (Matthew 13:13-15)

Check in with Mike Slaughter
From Chapter Four of *Renegade Gospel*

Sometimes the reason we do not see Jesus isn't our skepticism or intellectual doubt; it is because of our hardness of heart. When we cease to have our hearts broken by those tragedies, circumstances, and sufferings that break God's heart, when we fail to live more simply so that others may simply live, we are out of alignment with Christ, no longer in right relationship. We need to return to living and giving like God with skin on—Jesus.

Even though it's over a decade old, I still love the movie *Bruce Almighty*, starring Jim Carrey as down-on-his-luck news reporter Bruce Nolan and Morgan Freeman as God. When reporter Bruce is overlooked by his television station employer for a news anchor position that Bruce is convinced he deserved, he vehemently blames God for his misfortune. Morgan Freeman as God decides to do something about it and bequeaths the role of God to Bruce, humorously suggesting that perhaps Bruce will do a better job at it. Of course, after enjoying his new powers for a few days and improving his own life, Bruce begins to discover that the job is not nearly as easy or fulfilling as he had anticipated. Frustrated, Bruce consults with Morgan Freeman about how to make the whole thing work.

God tells him, "Parting your soup is not a miracle, Bruce. It's a magic trick. A single mom who's working two jobs and still finds time to take her kid to soccer practice, that's a miracle. A teenager who says 'no' to drugs and 'yes' to an education, that's a miracle. People want me to do everything for them. But what they don't realize is 'they' have the power. You want to see a miracle, son? Be the miracle."

Bruce protests, "What if I need you? What if I have questions?"

God smiles and answers, "That's your problem, Bruce. That's everybody's problem. You keep looking up."[4]

God's lines strike me each time I watch the movie. If we want to see a miracle, we need to **be** the miracle. Bruce's problem—the problem we all have—is that we keep looking up. We are trying to find Jesus in the extraordinary instead of the ordinary. That is why we miss him.

Go Deeper

1. Do you spend time in prayer or Bible study regularly? What is your daily prayer practice? How does that help you see Jesus?
2. Look at Matthew 25:6-12:

    "At midnight the cry rang out: 'Here's the bridegroom! Come out to meet him!'

    "Then all the virgins woke up and trimmed their lamps. The foolish ones said to the wise, 'Give us some of your oil; our lamps are going out.'

    "'No,' they replied, 'there may not be enough for both us and you. Instead, go to those who sell oil and buy some for yourselves.'

    "But while they were on their way to buy the oil, the bridegroom arrived. The virgins who were ready went in with him to the wedding banquet. And the door was shut.

    "Later the others also came. 'Lord, Lord,' they said, 'open the door for us!'

    "But he replied, 'Truly I tell you, I don't know you.'"

3. What does this parable teach us about expecting Jesus?
4. What would it mean for us to keep our lamps trimmed and our oil full today?
5. Look at John 14:15-17:

    "If you love me, keep my commands. And I will ask the Father, and he will give you another advocate to help you and be with you forever—the Spirit of truth. The world cannot accept him, because it neither sees him nor knows him. But you know him, for he lives with you and will be in you."

6. How does this passage encourage us to see Jesus?
7. Mike Slaughter wrote:

Be prepared. When you get serious about Jesus Christ and your life mission, he will completely mess up your life along with any preconceived notions you may have about how things are supposed to be. But, in this very disruption, it is also how you meet, experience, and follow Jesus in the world today.

8. How has Jesus messed up your life so far in your walk with him?
9. What preconceived notions have you had about following Jesus? How did those notions work out for you?
10. Look at the following passage from Matthew 25:34-40:

"Then the King will say to those on his right, 'Come, you who are blessed by my Father; take your inheritance, the kingdom prepared for you since the creation of the world. For I was hungry and you gave me something to eat, I was thirsty and you gave me something to drink, I was a stranger and you invited me in, I needed clothes and you clothed me, I was sick and you looked after me, I was in prison and you came to visit me'

"Then the righteous will answer him, 'Lord, when did we see you hungry and feed you, or thirsty and give you something to drink? When did we see you a stranger and invite you in, or needing clothes and clothe you? When did we see you sick or in prison and go to visit you?'

"The King will reply, 'Truly I tell you, whatever you did for one of the least of these brothers and sisters of mine, you did for me.'"

11. How are you challenged by these words? What do you need to regroup, reprioritize, or refocus in order to see Jesus more clearly in your life?

Make a Jesus Mural

Reflect on how Jesus is calling you to follow him more closely. Spend some time in personal reflection, using the suggestions below. Then grab some spray paint or markers and add to the mural. Use some of the words and images you listed here on the mural.

- Review Matthew 25 and look for words and phrases that teach us to see Jesus.
- Review John 14 and write down any words that point to the ability to see Jesus and the life he calls us to.

Listen for God

"I pray that the God of our Lord Jesus Christ, the Father of glory, will give you a spirit of wisdom and revelation that makes God known to you. I pray that the eyes of your heart will have enough light to see what is the hope of God's call, what is the richness of God's glorious inheritance among believers, and what is the overwhelming greatness of God's power that is working among us believers." Amen. (Ephesians 1:17-19 CEB)

5.

THE WAY OF
THE CROSS

"Whoever wants to be my disciple must deny themselves and take up their cross daily and follow me. For whoever wants to save their life will lose it, but whoever loses their life for me will save it. What good is it for someone to gain the whole world, and yet lose or forfeit their very self?" (Luke 9:23-25)

5.

THE WAY OF
THE CROSS

Watch the Video (Optional)

If your group is using the *Renegade Gospel* DVD, watch the DVD segment for Session 5, titled "The Way of the Cross." Then reflect on the following questions and make some notes. If you are in a group setting, use the questions to discuss the video.

Share in Conversation

1. Have you ever given up anything for Lent, such as sugar or soda? What was that experience like?

2. Why do you think we sometimes give up things for the Lenten season?

3. What are the things in your life for which you'd say you are "all in"?

4. What things do you give the most of your time and energy to?

Read and Reflect

Have you ever wondered what Lent is and where it came from? You don't see any passages about Lent in the Bible or hear of Jesus teaching about it anywhere, so why do we practice what seems like such a depressing, somber season? Well, the truth is that there is no spiritual law saying we should practice Lent. We are not required to give anything up for Lent in order to be a super Christian. There's nothing magical about it. But there is definitely something instructive and renewing about it.

Lent is the six weeks or forty days leading up to Easter, excluding Sundays, beginning with Ash Wednesday and ending on Easter. It is an ancient tradition of the church in which followers of Jesus practice self-denial, self-examination, and reflection on their walk with Jesus. It's a time of taking a hard look at our spiritual lives, inviting the Spirit to draw near to us as we draw near to Christ. I don't know about you, but I can get caught up in my own world. I've got lots of distractions—deadlines and commitments, activities and parties, sports and music practice, even church stuff—and at times I lose sight of my relationship with Jesus and my availability to his voice.

In the same way that Jesus walked the Jerusalem road all the way to his death on a cross, we walk through Lent, considering his sacrifice on our behalf and our commitment to his gospel. Taking the way of the cross means putting Jesus first and making sure nothing gets in the way of his priority in our lives. Our passions, our work, our friends, even our families have to come under his authority in our lives. When we say yes to Jesus' invitation to follow him, we are called to be like the good Samaritan in Luke 10, who crossed boundaries and borders to care for a dying man. When we say yes to Jesus' invitation to take the way of the cross, we are challenged like the rich young man in Luke 18 to sell everything we have and give it to the poor. When we say yes to Jesus' invitation to carry our cross, we are told it will mean dropping everything—no excuses—and following Jesus.

So Lent is a season for us to examine our walk with Jesus and see if we are traveling the revolutionary way with him or if we are playing it safe and just hanging out in our sanctuaries. Following the way of the cross means that the things that break God's heart break our hearts. It means that the things God cares about are the things we care about. It means that the places Jesus went are the places we are called to go. If we truly examine our walk with Jesus, it may be very helpful to do some kind of fasting or to give something up.

Lenten sacrifice helps us create space in our minds, our hearts, and our lives so we can really see, hear, and understand what God is telling us. We might give up coffee, sugar, or television, or we might take on a new practice such as getting up early for morning prayer or giving away anything we have too much of. These acts of sacrifice help us deny ourselves and take up the cross of Jesus. We ask ourselves: Does our faith walk match up with our faith talk? How are we doing at this life-with-Jesus thing? In what ways do we need the Spirit to help us adjust our lives so that we become more and more like Jesus?

Scripture Focus

Large crowds were traveling with Jesus, and turning to them he said: "If anyone comes to me and does not hate father and mother, wife and children, brothers and sisters—yes, even their own life— such a person cannot be my disciple. And whoever does not carry their cross and follow me cannot be my disciple." (Luke 14:25-27)

Check in with Mike Slaughter
From Chapter Five of *Renegade Gospel*

Can I be honest with you? I am one of those who struggle with materialism. All of us grow accustomed to the comforts that we insulate ourselves with, comforts that seem to grow with the passage of time. . . .

It is so easy to seek the gifts of God rather than the God who gives. Our expectations grow with income and age. The 36-inch color TV still works fine, but a 52-inch flatscreen is so much better, especially when expertly installed with surround sound. Materialism continues to slither forward, thanks to the engineered obsolescence of our smartphones, tablets, and laptops. . . .

Following Jesus in the way of the cross will mean a radical reordering of our priorities. We get a glimpse of those priorities in two of Jesus' parables. In Luke 10:25-37, Jesus told the story of a good Samaritan who sacrifices his time and financial resources to help an unknown stranger. "Go and do likewise," Jesus commanded a Jewish expert in the Law. In Luke 12:13-21, Jesus related the parable of a rich man who forgets his responsibility to be a channel for God's blessings in helping the least and the lost. The man in the story wastes his precious gift of life, living only to serve his expanding lust for bigger, better, and more. Jesus told him, "'You fool! This very night your life will be demanded from you. Then who will get what you have prepared for yourself?' This is how it will be with whoever stores up things for themselves but is not rich toward God" (verses 20-21). What a poignant reminder—the only thing we can take with us beyond death is what we do for God and others. . . .

Following Jesus means being "rich toward God" by serving God's interests in meeting others' needs. Jesus put it this way in one of his parables: "I tell you, use worldly wealth to gain friends for yourselves, so that when it is gone, you will be welcomed into eternal dwellings" (Luke 16:9). The rebel Jesus calls us to use our affluence for the purpose of influence in the lives of people who have neither.

Go Deeper

1. What do you think it means to "take up your cross"?
2. Look at Luke 12:35-36:

> "Be dressed ready for service and keep your lamps burning, like servants waiting for their master to return from a wedding banquet, so that when he comes and knocks they can immediately open the door for him."

3. In the words of Jesus above, who do you think the master is? Who are the servants?

4. Why do you think this Bible verse is emphasized during the season of Lent?
5. What would it mean for us to keep our lamps trimmed and our oil full today?
6. Look at Philippians 2:5-8:

In your relationships with one another, have the same mindset as Christ Jesus:

Who, being in very nature God,
    did not consider equality with God something to be used to
    his own advantage;
rather, he made himself nothing
    by taking the very nature of a servant,
    being made in human likeness.
And being found in appearance as a man,
    he humbled himself
    by becoming obedient to death—
        even death on a cross!

7. Summarize the "mindset" of Christ described in the passage.
8. What would it mean for us to take on that same mindset?
9. In the words below from Luke 14:25-27, what do you think Jesus means by "hating father and mother"?

Large crowds were traveling with Jesus, and turning to them he said: "If anyone comes to me and does not hate father and mother, wife and children, brothers and sisters—yes, even their own life— such a person cannot be my disciple. And whoever does not carry their cross and follow me cannot be my disciple."

10. Here's what Mike Slaughter wrote about the above passage:

Obviously Jesus didn't really want us to hate those closest to us. But he was saying that our love and allegiance to him must supersede and take precedence over all other relationships, even those with our families.

11. How difficult is it to put Jesus first, above every other relationship or commitment? What are some real-life examples of putting Jesus first?
12. How are you challenged by today's discussion? How can you follow Jesus more closely in your life?

Make a Jesus Mural

Reflect on how Jesus is calling you to follow him more closely. Spend some time in personal reflection, using the questions below. Then grab some spray paint or markers and add to the mural. Use some of the words and images you listed here on the mural.

- Review Luke 10:25-37 and list some words that describe what this story says about the way of the cross.
- Review Luke 9:57-62 and list more words that describe what Jesus' teaching says about the way of the cross.
- Review John 15:9-17. List more words that describe the way of Jesus.

Listen for God

Lord Jesus, your way calls us to sacrifice and love as you have sacrificed for us and loved us. Use these days of Lent to clear out everything that gets in the way of our love for you and our willingness to say yes to your way. Thank you for the cross. Thank you for inviting us to walk the way of the cross with you. Give us courage, strength, and grace to follow you wherever you lead. Amen.

6.

RESURRECTION

But if it is preached that Christ has been raised from the dead, how can some of you say that there is no resurrection of the dead? If there is no resurrection of the dead, then not even Christ has been raised. And if Christ has not been raised, our preaching is useless and so is your faith. (1 Corinthians 15:12-14)

6.

RESURRECTION

Watch the Video (Optional)

If your group is using the *Renegade Gospel* DVD, watch the DVD segment for Session 6, titled "Resurrection." Then reflect on the following questions and make some notes. If you are in a group setting, use the questions to discuss the video.

Share in Conversation

1. What are some modern-day myths that some people believe in and others doubt?
2. Would you call yourself more of a doubter or someone who can entertain crazy possibilities?
3. When have you doubted any aspects of the Christian faith?
4. How often do you swing back and forth between faith and doubt? How does it feel, and what do you do?

Read and Reflect

Let's face it: the resurrection of Jesus is a tough thing to accept blindly without any doubt or questions. We believe Jesus was born into the world, walked among us, and died a terrible death on a cross. We believe there were crowds of credible witnesses to his death. But the empty tomb? The resurrected Jesus? That can be a stretch for our small minds, even though he appeared to witnesses on several different occasions. Somehow, even with the witnesses and the multiple appearances, there is more room to doubt that part of Jesus' story. It takes a leap of faith. The Resurrection was probably the most astonishing claim made by the disciples, and even today the church stands on that one claim made thousands of years ago.

Every bit of the Christian church in the world today is based on the claim that Jesus was raised from the dead. There is no Christian church without the Resurrection. On the Day of Pentecost, Peter preached a sermon to the crowd proclaiming to all the fact that "God has raised this Jesus to life, and we are all witnesses of it" (Acts 2:32). Everything from Acts to Revelation to our church communities today hinges on God raising Jesus to life. In 1 Corinthians 15, Paul says that without the Resurrection our faith is useless, that the disciples are false witnesses, and that we are still living in our sin. The resurrection of Jesus is everything to his followers. It's what we believe and who we are—Easter people, who believe that God makes beauty from ashes, life from death, hope from despair.

Think about it: if our beliefs about Jesus were easy, if all of it were all black and white, we'd have no need for faith. Faith is the thing that holds together our doubts and beliefs. When we get to the end of our knowledge and ability to understand, faith gets us to a point of claiming the supernatural work of God in our lives. And you know what? We don't need much faith for God to do great things in us. Jesus said, "If you have faith as small as a mustard seed, you can say to this mulberry tree, 'Be uprooted and planted in the sea,' and it will obey you" (Luke 17:6). Just a little faith can move us from doubt and unbelief to belief and faith—and with our little bit of faith, God does amazing things!

Staking our lives on the truth of Jesus' resurrection means that we believe God can do more than we can ask, believe, or imagine. It means seeing the world through the eyes of faith, with the perspective of complete possibility. It means asking ourselves what God can do in and through us with our mustard-seed faith. Impossible things are possible with God.

Scripture Focus

For what I received I passed on to you as of first importance: that Christ died for our sins according to the Scriptures, that he was buried, that he was raised on the third day according to the Scriptures, and that he appeared to Cephas, and then to the Twelve. After that, he appeared to more than five hundred of the brothers and sisters at the same time, most of whom are still living, though some have fallen asleep. (1 Corinthians 15:3-6)

Check in with Mike Slaughter
From Chapter Six of *Renegade Gospel*

This faith-doubt struggle seems to have been normative for many of Jesus' first disciples. We are told in Matthew's Gospel that, following the Resurrection, "the eleven disciples went to Galilee, to the mountain where Jesus had told them to go. When they saw him, they worshiped him; but some doubted" (Matthew 28:16-17). We read in Luke's account that Jesus appeared to the disciples, who had barricaded themselves behind locked doors, fearing the authorities' retribution after witnessing the execution of the one they believed to be Israel's deliverer. "Why are you troubled, and why do doubts rise in your minds? Look at my hands and my feet. It is I myself! Touch me and see; a ghost does not have flesh and bones, as you see I have" (Luke 24:38-39). Even when they were witnessing the Resurrection miracle, the disciples struggled with doubt! . . .

After I encountered the resurrected rebel Jesus, he gave me new eyes with which to see. I identify with the blind man Jesus healed on the sabbath in John 9, which caused consternation among the self-righteously religious Pharisees. When the healed man was brought before the religious authorities for questioning, he defiantly declared in verse 25: "One thing I do know. I was blind but now I see!" I, too, was once blind and now I see. I am a firsthand witness to the power of the resurrected Christ as I assess how he has transformed the way I see myself and others.

Before Jesus, I defined myself by my limitations. I remember telling my parents on more than one occasion about my academic struggles, "I can't help it. I'm stupid." Once I met the resurrected Jesus, however, I felt reassured that I was God's masterpiece, created new in Christ Jesus so I could "do the good things he planned for us long ago" (Ephesians 2:10 NLT).

Go Deeper

1. Why is the Resurrection so important to the Christian faith?
2. Look at Matthew 28:16-17 and Luke 24:38-39:

"The eleven disciples went to Galilee, to the mountain where Jesus had told them to go. When they saw him, they worshiped him; but some doubted."

"Why are you troubled, and why do doubts rise in your minds? Look at my hands and my feet. It is I myself! Touch me and see; a ghost does not have flesh and bones, as you see I have."

3. How are you encouraged by the fact that the disciples had doubts?
4. The Letter of James says that faith is not just about overcoming unbelief but is meant to be put into action. Look at these verses from James:

Do not merely listen to the word, and so deceive yourselves. Do what it says (1:22).

What good is it, my brothers and sisters, if someone claims to have faith but has no deeds? Can such a faith save them? Suppose a brother or a sister is without clothes and daily food. If one of you says to them, "Go in peace; keep warm and well fed," but does nothing about their physical needs, what good is it? In the same way, faith by itself, if it is not accompanied by action, is dead (2:14-17).

Show me your faith without deeds, and I will show you my faith by my deeds. You believe that there is one God. Good! Even the demons believe that—and shudder" (2:18-19).

5. What is the relationship between our faith and our actions?
6. Believing that God can do amazing things in and through you, how can you live more fully?
7. What does it mean to stake your life on the resurrection of Jesus?
8. How are you challenged by today's discussion?

Make a Jesus Mural

Reflect on the significance of Jesus' resurrection. Spend some time in personal reflection, using the questions below. Then grab some spray paint or markers and add to the mural. Use some of the words and images you listed here on the mural. Hang the mural in the youth room, and remember this journey of discovering the rebel Jesus. When you wonder who Jesus is, take a look at your mural to remind you who he is and the life he has called you to.

- Review 1 Corinthians 15 and list some words that describe what this story says about the significance of the Resurrection.
- Review Luke 24 and look for parts of the story you've never noticed before. Pay attention to what God is teaching you about his power to do more than you can imagine.

Listen for God

Lord, by no means do I fully comprehend who you are. But I commit today to give my life to you, not just in words but in action. With all my flaws, I accept your love and forgiveness, and I give it to others. I pledge my allegiance to the rebel Jesus and commit myself to the renegade gospel. Not my will but your will be done. In Jesus' name. Amen.

NOTES

1. Spurgeon, Charles, http://www.christianfaith.com/christian-quotes/.

2. Sitkoff, Harvard, *King: Pilgrimage to the Mountaintop* (New York: Hill and Wang, 2008), 208.

3. From *The United Methodist Hymnal* (Nashville: The United Methodist Publishing House, 1989), 882.

4. *Bruce Almighty*, Universal Studios, 2003; http://www.imdb.com/title/tt0315327/quotes.

CPSIA information can be obtained at www.ICGtesting.com
Printed in the USA
LVOW10s2355160915

454164LV00007BA/24/P

9 781426 792830